SUBMARINE
1901 - 2001

A WARSHIPS IFR SPECIAL PUBLICATION TO MARK THE CENTENARY OF THE ROYAL NAVY'S SUBMARINE SERVICE.

Featuring Specially Selected Images From The Goodman Collection

PICTURED: Holland 4 ɛ of the 20th Century. ł as a gunnery target. P

CW00686906

CONTENTS

ABOVE: The Swiftsure Class nuclear-powered attack boat HMS Splendid arriving at Liverpool in 1984. Fifteen years later she became the first British submarine to fire cruise missiles in anger when she attacked Serb targets as part of NATO's Operation Allied Force. Photo: Dave Cullen.

A MOMENTOUS CENTURY

FOREWORD BY REAR ADMIRAL R.P. STEVENS CB, The Flag Officer Submarines

The commissioning of Holland I on October 2 1901 set in train a series of events which has had an impact on so many lives. That day also saw the beginning of an illustrious record which we are now commemorating in the centenary year of the Royal Navy Submarine Service. The past century has seen the British submarine metamorphose from the 'Cinderella' of the fleet to a prized power projection asset that is fully integrated into our battlegroup structures.

The rich tapestry of the histories of the people who have carried out that transformation, their bravery, dedication and sacrifice, has been recorded many times elsewhere. It is fitting that this publication should complement those accounts with its depiction of the cornucopia of hardware British submariners have had at their disposal over the past century.

It is also fitting that it pays attention to the genesis of the submersible in use from the days of sail until Holland I made its cautious entry onto the stage of maritime operations. On the pages which follow we go from early experimentation to the technical complexity, immense capability and huge potential of our modern flotilla. In illustrating the kind of submarines the Royal Navy has deployed, and continues to deploy, all over the world, a momentous portrait is created.

PAYING FREEDOM'S PRICE:

HMS Porpoise was a minelaying submarine completed in the early 1930s. She could carry 50 conventional mines. She was sunk in January 1945, possibly by a Japanese aircraft, while laying mines off Penang.
Photo: Goodman Collection.

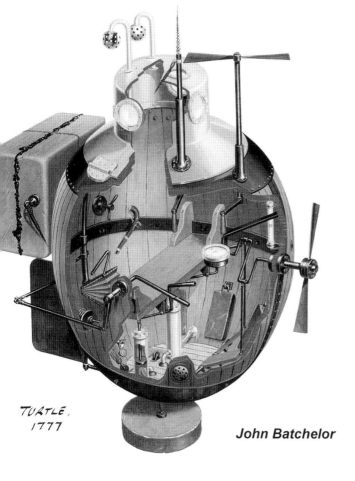

TURTLE, 1777

John Batchelor

EARLY DISASTERS FAILED TO SINK A GOOD IDEA

Submersibles have been lurking around under the waves, in one form or another, since the Middle Ages. A German inventor created a diving boat as far back as 1465, but by the 16th Century it was the English who were leading research into such vessels.

Early submersibles were often made by placing an upturned hull on top of another and were powered by oars. Their unfortunate crews had to rely on the air trapped between the hulls for survival beneath the waves.

Not surprisingly they were not very successful, although some of the early submarines managed to stay under for a while and cover short distances. Too often the early experiments ended in disaster. One such tragedy happened in the summer of 1774. A Norfolk shipwright called Day brought a submersible boat he had constructed to the South West of England, having already managed to descend to a depth of 30ft off

the coast of East Anglia. His intention was to use the great naval and ship-building port of Plymouth to take his experiments even further. After a well executed shallow dive in Plymouth Sound, Day should have stopped to consider what he had discovered. However, he was tempted by an offer of money to take his submersible down further. So, entering the air chamber of the vessel, and putting on extra ballast, in the form of stones in special holders bolted to its exterior, Day cheerfully descended again. But, on reaching a depth of over a hundred feet beneath the Sound, the fledgling submariner discovered something he had hitherto been ignorant of - the ability of water pressure to crush his vessel. He perished as it imploded.

In the late 1700s other primitive submersibles were built despite this disaster, including the Turtle which was used during the American War of Independence

by rebels who tried, and failed, to sink British warships (*see our picture, left*).

In 1801 the Admiralty financed the first successful underwater operations by paying the turncoat inventor Robert Fulton to attack the French fleet. An American, Fulton had emigrated to France in 1797, where, with a grant from Napoleon, he built his Nautilus submarine in five months.

This vessel was close to a modern submarine in that it had a conning tower, diving planes and flooding valves. With space for a crew of three men, Nautilus was designed for a depth of 25ft. She needed to be in a position directly beneath a target ship's hull, in order to place a buoyant explosive charge. Although given assistance by the host navy, Fulton's invention was considered an "infernal machine" by many French Admirals.

Disgusted at lack of progress due to this mistrust, Fulton changed sides and took his idea to the British. Although the British Government was very interested, and supported further tests, the Royal Navy expressed a similar revulsion to the French admirals, and so, for the moment, the pursuit of submarine warfare collapsed. However, more war-fighting submersibles appeared in the American Civil War of the 1860s, with the desperate Confederates

launching the highly advanced, but dangerously unreliable, Hunley against the Union Navy, which was blockading Charleston. The Confederate submariners claimed the first ever sinking of a surface ship by a submerged vessel - the USS Housatonic - in 1864. Subsequently the designer and builder of the submarine, James McClintock, was smuggled to Nova Scotia, headquarters of the British Commander-in-Chief North America, where he was debriefed by British naval officers. Their favourable report, with McClintock's drawings and description of the Hunley, were eventually to influence British submarine policy.

ONE of the first submarines to be built in Britain was the Resurgam, which made her debut at a Liverpool ship-builders' in 1879. She was powered by steam on the surface and, while submerged, used the latent heat of the boiler to push herself along. However, this design was not very successful, being unable to keep down due to the manner in which the diving planes were fitted.

In the 1880s and 1890s the French Navy enjoyed some success in submarine experiments. Noting the success of these, the British properly entered the submarine arms race at the turn of the century.

An American Civil War submersible.

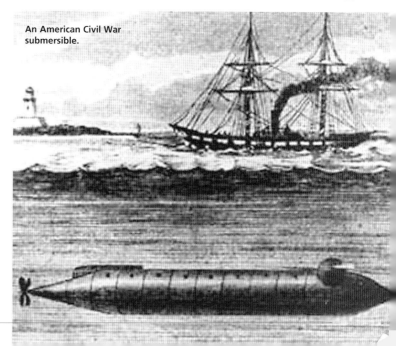

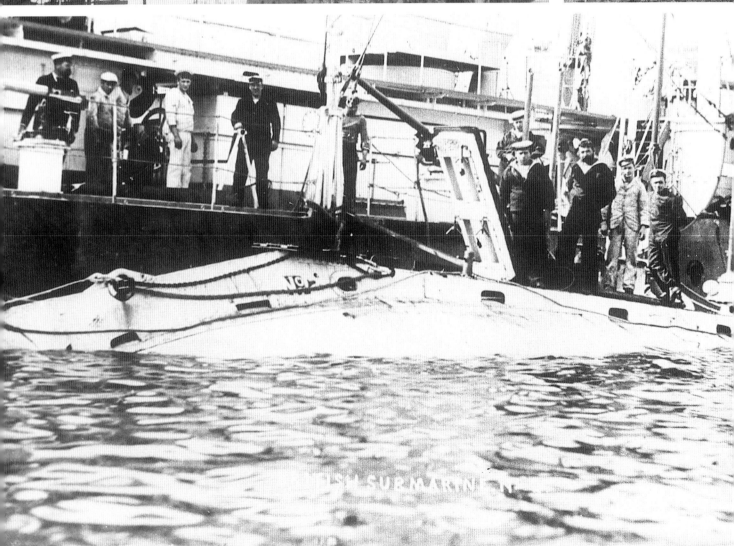

IRISH SUBMARINE

The Royal Navy gave the go-ahead in 1901 to buy five Holland Class submarines, costing £175,000. They were to be built under licence by Vickers & Son and Maxim Ltd, at Barrow-in-Furness, in the firm's Devonshire Docks. The same site is now used to construct the latest nuclear submarines. Holland I was laid down in February 1901, launched in November of that year and started sea trials in January 1902. She had a tiny conning tower, which barely poked above the waves, and displaced 122 tons submerged. Her overall length of 63' 10" only enabled her to have one torpedo tube. Her main power plant was a petrol engine for sailing on the surface, where she could vent the fumes, and electric batteries for silent running under the water. She could manage a maximum of eight knots on the surface and around seven knots submerged.

It is worth digressing here to note, that, in 1913, while being towed to the breaker's yard,

Holland I sank off Plymouth. In 1981 her location off the Eddystone Light was pin-pointed. She was raised by the Royal Navy and is today a star exhibit at the RN Submarine Museum in Gosport.

WHEN the first Holland boat was commissioned into the fleet submariners and their vessels were regarded with suspicion by some officers in the RN.

However, while it makes a good story, no one actually said they were "underhand and damned un-English". Successful sea trials with the Hollands warranted ordering a new class of submarines which were basically an improved version of the American-designed boats. Between 1902 and 1905 the Admiralty built 13 A Class submarines. The final boat, A13, was 105' 6" long, with a beam of 12' 8". She had a displacement of 190 tons surfaced and 205 tons submerged. She was also fitted with two 18-inch tubes and car-

ried four torpedoes. The last A boat remained in service with the RN until 1920 and was notable for having pioneered diesel engines. The B and C Class submarines quickly followed, both with a beam of 13' 7". All were very similar, though the Bs and Cs, at 142' in length, were longer than the A Class boats. The main enhancement embodied by the Bs was a more substantial deck casing which improved surface performance and enabled a bigger reserve of buoyancy.

They were also fitted with a pair of hydroplanes at the forward end of the conning tower to improve underwater handling - a first for the Royal Navy and an innovation which was not repeated until 50 years later when it was re-introduced in US nuclear submarines. Thirty eight of the small C Class coastal defence boats were built between 1906 and 1910.

Four of them were sent to the Baltic in 1916. *See our picture and accompanying caption on P10 for more detail.* Another C

CLOCKWISE: A Holland Class boat is lifted high into the air by a crane at Portsmouth Dockyard in the early 1900s; a trio of Holland boats nestled alongside their depot ship, HMS Hazard; a tight shot of Holland 2 moored alongside a depot ship - possibly HMS Hazard again - her crew posing on the casing. Photos: Goodman Collection.

Class boat was sacrificed at Zeebrugge on St George's Day 1918, when she was packed with explosives and used to blow up the viaduct connecting the mole to the shore. *See the inside front cover of this publication.* Chatham Dockyard built some of the Cs, partly to end Vickers' monopoly of the technology and partly because the Barrow yard could not keep up with the Admiralty's demand for more and more submarines.

ABOVE: An A Class boat in Portsmouth Harbour around 1909. BELOW: HMS Victory features in the background as HMS A13 leaves Portsmouth. This submarine pioneered diesel engines in the Royal Navy. An experimental diesel engine was fitted in A13 following an explosion in A5 caused by petrol vapour. Diesel has a higher flash point than petrol and is therefore safer. Submarines with petrol engines customarily carried white mice which started squeaking in an alarming fashion if they inhaled carbon monoxide, so giving crews early warning. Photos: Goodman Collection.

ABOVE: C12 pictured at Torquay pre-WW1. BELOW: C12, C13, B1, C14, C18 and B4 rafted up. In late 1913, C14 sank in Plymouth Sound following a collision with another vessel. Remarkably there was no loss of life and she was raised to the surface and repaired at Devonport Dockyard. C12, C13 and C14 had airlocks fitted in 1908 in an effort to give their crews some means of escape in event of an emergency. Photos: Goodman Collection.

FIRST BLOOD IS DRAWN IN WW1

WITH the experience of three classes of submarines, the Admiralty felt confident enough to build a fourth, larger class. The D Class boats were the first British submarines intended for overseas operations, and were nearly twice as large as their predecessors.

Apart from the introduction of diesels, most of the advances stemmed from an increase in displacement. Greater internal volume and a larger crew lightened the workload on long patrols.

Diesel engines eliminated the dangerous petrol vapour which had caused numerous explosions in the early boats. Saddle tanks increased internal space, while twin screws gave greater manoeuvrability.

The Ds were also the first British boats which could send and receive radio messages, though the extendible mast had to be rigged by hand. In another innovation, D4 was the first submarine to be fitted with a gun. In 1910 the Admiralty ordered six improved Ds.

THE E Class boats which came next were 181' long, but had only single bow and stern tubes. The diesels were the, by now standard, Vickers 4-stroke type. The Es also had two watertight bulkheads.

The design proved highly successful and production continued right through to 1917. They would bear the brunt of the Allies' submarine offensive in WW1, scoring some of the outstanding successes of the war in the Sea of Marmora and the Baltic, but losing over a half of their number. The improved Es were three feet longer and had two bow tubes. The forward bulkhead was moved to ease torpedo loading, the engine position was also altered, the conning tower enlarged and a third bulkhead was introduced.

ON the outbreak of war in 1914 production of improved Es, to a standard design from Chatham Dockyard, had been diversified around the country.

The submarine service which would wield the Es so effectively was an an elite force. It attracted many young officers eager for the prospect of early command. However, the war started with a curious reversal of fortune. With the German fleet and merchant shipping mostly swept from the seas, the large and modern British submarine fleet could find few targets and the enemy was to score the first notable killer blow.

IN Germany, Tirpitz at first rejected what he rudely called 'kleinkreig' - small war - but the Kaiser's U-boats swiftly proved themselves. The first warship to be sunk in the open sea was HMS Pathfinder, by U-21. This had minimal impact on British sweeps across the North Sea, but, when Lt Horton in E9 sank the cruiser Hela the Germans withdrew into the Baltic. Then U-9 sank three elderly British cruisers off the Hook of Holland, and the Royal Navy lost 1,459 men, most of them recently called-up reservists. The incident also, temporarily, drove the Grand Fleet out of Scapa Flow to the west coast of Scotland at Lough Swilly.

BRITISH submarine operations in the Baltic achieved some notable successes, but communication with the Russians made life difficult. After the Bolshevik seizure of power the RN's submarines were scuttled in their Baltic base ports and their crews returned home. In the Mediterranean submarines were sent to reinforce the faltering

LEFT: HMS E4 saw service in the North Sea during WW1, snooping around off German naval bases. During the Battle of Heligoland Bight in August 1914, she braved enemy fire to rescue British sailors, who had been dropped in a small boat to pick up survivors from German ships, but then found themselves stranded when the enemy chased off their own vessel. E4 met a tragic end, sinking with all hands in August 1916, after colliding with submarine E41.
Photo: Goodman Collection.

ABOVE: The Australian submarine HMAS AE2 saw service mainly in the Mediterranean during WW1 and, under the command of Lieutenant Commander Henry Stoker RN, breached the Dardanelles in April 1915. Although she sank a Turkish gunboat, she was herself driven to destruction by Turkish gunboats in the Sea of Marmara not long after.
Photo: Royal Australian Navy.

Allied attack on the Dardanelles. Lieutenant Holbrook, in the primitive B11, scored a first when he sank the old Turkish battleship Messudieh off Constantinople in December 1914, and so won the first Victoria Cross awarded to a member of the RN submarine service. Then, in May 1915, Lieutenant Commanders Boyle, in E14, and Nasmith, in E11, both won VCs for their efforts. The Germans, however, retaliated by sending the U-21 from the North Sea to sink the two old battleships Triumph and Majestic.

AFTER many months of stalemate, which saw the Germans increasingly sinking ships without warning, in defiance of the rules of war, unrestricted U-boat warfare broke out in February 1917.

In that month the Germans sank an average of over three ships a day, totalling 105 ships (over 300,000 tons) with the loss of 400 merchant seamen.

Allied losses continued at a horrendous, but declining, rate for the rest of the war as the British reverted to the convoy system they had used so successfully in previous major wars.

The Germans had found a weapon with which they thought they could impose a blockade on the British Isles. They came perilously close to success, but, in the end, over 200 German submarines were sunk and they failed to achieve their objective.

THE Royal Navy had started the war with 72 boats, representing a force bigger in numbers and more technologically advanced than any other submarine force. By the end of the war, the Royal Navy's submarine flotilla numbered 142 boats which were divided into 14 classes.

The RN had also gained a proud, new tradition: When Horton returned to Harwich from his successful patrol with E9 in September 1914 he had flown a skull and crossbones flag to indicate the sinking of an enemy warship.

RIGHT: In late summer 1916, the Royal Navy decided to send four C Class coastal submarines - C26, C27, C32 and C35 - to operate as a detached squadron supporting the Russians in the Baltic. To avoid having to run the gauntlet of the narrow straits at the entrance to the Baltic, which were, naturally, infested with German naval forces, the C Class boats were towed to Archangel in the Russian north.

They were then put on barges and transported to Petrograd by inland waterways, arriving on the Neva less than three weeks after leaving the UK. This remarkable photograph shows one of the C Class boats on a Russian barge en-route from the White Sea to the Baltic (note the tiller man well clad against the cold). Photo: Goodman Collection.

OPPOSITE, MIDDLE: C38 leaving Portsmouth. In 1911, C38 (together with sister vessels C36 and C37) made an epic 72 day voyage to Hong Kong. All three stayed on the surface throughout and were only towed part of the way. C38 stayed there throughout WW1 and was sent to the breaker's yard in 1919. OPPOSITE, BOTTOM: C34, one of the later C Class boats (and therefore displaying full-length casing). She fell victim of a torpedo from a German submarine while patrolling off Fair Isle in the summer of 1917. Photos: Goodman Collection.
BELOW: A rare picture of the Australian submarine AE2 on her way north through the Suez Canal to her date with destiny - and destruction - in the Dardanelles (see P9).
Photo: Royal Australian Navy.

ABOVE, RIGHT: A good view of the 4-inch gun of HMAS J7, which was mounted on a raised platform. Built at Devonport Dockyard, she was laid down in August 1916 and completed in November 1917. After service with the Grand Fleet in the later stages of the war, the seven large and swift J Class submarines were transferred to Australia in 1919.
Having needed considerable refitting to keep them operational, the J Class boats were thought too expensive for Australia's modest naval budget and so, starting in August 1921, were retired from service. Photo: Royal Australian Navy.

BELOW: J7 about to be launched from Devonport's famed covered slipway. Photo: Goodman Collection.

HMS J7 slides into the Tamar at Devonport. Photo: Goodman Collection.

BELOW: HMS K8 was a member of the ill-fated K Class. Entering service from 1916, the steam-powered K Class boats were extremely fast thanks to their boilers, which required funnels. Not a good idea in a submarine, the funnels necessitated a complex process to ensure they were properly folded down and sealed before diving. The consequences if they were not are easy to imagine. The time taken to dive was painful, and potentially fatal with German aircraft on the hunt. It took five minutes, as against 30 seconds by other WW1 British boats. During submerging trials at Devonport one member of the class refused to surface for no obvious reason for several hours. In service with the Grand Fleet they proved equally jinxed. During the so-called 'Battle of May Island', in January 1918, ten K boats took part in a night exercise which saw a series of collisions between the submarines at high speed. A cruiser and a battle-cruiser also collided with K boats. The end result was two K boats lost with all hands - K4 and K17 - and various others badly damaged. It was once observed that K Class submarines had "the speed of a destroyer, the turning circle of a battle-cruiser and the bridge control equipment of a picket boat." Eight weeks before the disaster at May Island K1 had been accidentally sunk off the coast of Denmark by the guns of a British warship. Most K boats had been broken up by the mid-1920s and to many it was a mystery why they persisted so long. Photo: Goodman Collection.

ABOVE & BELOW: Another innovative class of boats also dogged with bad luck. The M Class were an extraordinary concept, inspired by intelligence reports that the Germans were constructing U-boat cruisers armed with 5.9-inch guns. The British decided to go several better, creating the M Class, mounting 12-inch guns taken from redundant Majestic Class battleships.

M1 was the only member of the class to see service in WW1 and she was sent to the Mediterranean in the closing stages of the conflict to ready herself for a surprise bombardment mission against Constantinople.

The war ended before this could go ahead.

M1 was lost with all hands off Plymouth in late 1925, probably as a result of being hit by a surface vessel.

M2 had her 12-inch gun removed in October 1925 and a small hangar for an embarked seaplane was constructed. She was also lost with all hands in 1932, it is believed because water flooded into her hangar. M3 survived the longest, receiving a radical reconstruction to become a prototype minelayer submarine in 1927. Retired from service in spring 1932 she was scrapped the following year. M1 is pictured, above, while M3 is below, in her pre-1927 guise with 12-inch gun.

Photos: Goodman Collection.

ABOVE: American-designed during WW1, early examples of H Class submarines were assembled by Vickers at their Canadian yard using 'components' manufactured in America. This was necessary as America was still neutral. From 1917 H Class boats were also built in the USA. They were so effective they were to see service throughout the inter-war period and even into WW2 in a limited fashion. HMS H28 was not broken up until 1944. Photo: Goodman Collection.

BELOW: HMAS Oxley and sister vessel Otway, represented Australia's third ill-fated attempt to establish a submarine arm for its navy. Ordered in 1924 and completed in 1927, HMAS Oxley sailed for Australia in January 1928, arriving at Sydney in March the following year. However, the severe economic depression of the early 1930s led to both boats being paid off into reserve. They were re-activated in 1931 as Royal Navy vessels and went to the Mediterranean. Although placed in reserve again in the UK by the late 1930s, both Oxley and Otway were pressed into service when war with Germany loomed. Oxley was lost in an unfortunate incident when the RN boat Triton torpedoed her a week after the commencement of hostilities. Photo: Royal Australian Navy.

ABOVE:HMS X1 was not a successful hybrid, but she was the first new post-WW1 design of submarine in Britain. She was a massive vessel, displacing 2,780 tons surfaced and 3,600 tons submerged, and was armed with four 5.2-inch guns in two turrets plus six 21-inch torpedo tubes. Her machinery was prone to problems and she was put into reserve in 1930. See our article on P17. Photo: Goodman Collection.

BELOW: Built by Chatham Dockyard and launched in November 1931, the Swordfish Class submarine HMS Sturgeon was to be operated by the exiled Dutch naval forces between October 1943 and September 1945. She was the only one of a class of four to survive war service and was sent to the breakers in 1947.Seahorse was lost in December 1939, after hitting a mine, while Starfish was destroyed by the German vessel M7 on January 9 the following year. Patrols in the Heligoland Bight were abandoned not long after. Swordfish was lost in mysterious circumstances off St Catherine's Point in November 1940. Photo: Goodman Collection.

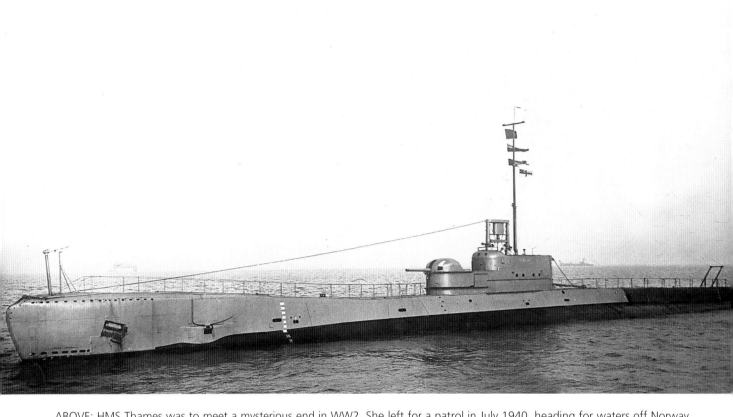

ABOVE: HMS Thames was to meet a mysterious end in WW2. She left for a patrol in July 1940, heading for waters off Norway and never returned. It is believed she hit a mine off Stavanger.

BELOW: HMS Thistle was to be sunk by a torpedo from U-4 off Skudenes in April 1940.

OPPOSITE: The Shark Class boat Sterlet pictured nearing completion in the late 1930s, having been built at Chatham Dockyard. She was sunk in April 1940 off the coast of Denmark by three German submarine-hunting trawlers.
Photos: Goodman Collection.

TWO DECADES
OF UNEASY PEACE

After WW1 there were many people who, mindful of the horrific nature of unrestricted U-boat war as practiced by the Germans, thought post-war peace conferences should outlaw submarines altogether. Not so the French, among them the would-be naval philosopher Castex who advocated a large submarine fleet as the perfect means to, finally, bridle British seapower. The British also wanted to preserve their submarine fleet but not at the cost of battleships and cruisers. Their negotiating position at the 1922 Washington naval conference, though often misunderstood, was to argue for parity in capital ships with the USA and embarrass the French by arguing overtly for the banning of submarines.

Though the E Class submarines had proved successful, and were the largest single class to be built, experiments with other types had already started by the end of WW1. Generally submarines grew larger from coastal and overseas types to fleet submarines, such as the K Class, *as mentioned earlier in this book*, mounting 4-inch and 3-inch guns, and, in the quest for speed, driven by steam turbines. They were not the first steam driven boats, having been preceded by HM Submarine Swordfish, also known as S1, which was scrapped after trials. As we have seen on earlier pages there were other experimental designs, most of them being of WW1 origin. Developments of what was soon recognised as the classic Holland, or single, hull and the Admiralty double hull and saddle tank designs, proved much more successful. During the inter-war years three basic submarine weapons solidified - the torpedo, the mine and the medium calibre gun. Diesel engines became the norm for propulsion. Submarine X1, when launched in 1923, was the largest submarine in the world and was termed a submarine cruiser (*see our picture and caption on P15*). Despite her bulk she was good at diving and was pretty agile. However, machinery problems fatally hampered her operational value. Several small classes of submarines were built between the wars. Some, like the Porpoise Class, were intended primarily as mine-layers.

The characteristic surface speed was about 15 knots and the submerged speed for short periods less than 10 knots, though even at two or three knots the submarine had an underwater endurance measured in hours rather than days.

The three large River Class boats built for the Royal Navy were the first diesel-powered boats to exceed 20 knots on the surface and were intended to accompany the fleet.

ABOVE: Built by Chatham Dockyard and launched in May 1934, HMS Shark was to meet her end off Norway on July 5 1940. She was pursued by German mine-sweeping trawlers and aircraft which depth-charged her. Badly damaged she had to be scuttled off Skudenes but was later raised and pressed into enemy service. With dimensions of 208' 9" (length) and 24' (beam), her displacement was 670 tons surfaced and 960 tons submerged. An S Class submarine, she was armed with a 3-inch gun and six 21-inch torpedo tubes. Photo: Goodman Collection.

BELOW: Alongside at HMS Dolphin in Gosport is the submarine HMS L27, which was lucky to return from a WW2 patrol in which she was rammed by a German warship. The L27 torpedoed a 7,000 ton merchant vessel off Cherbourg on October 15 1940 and then found herself run-down by an angry escort vessel. The incident was the only sinking by torpedo achieved by any L Class submarine in WW2 as the Ls were principally employed in training. Forty L Class submarines were built for the Royal Navy between 1917 and 1920. Their armament was a 4-inch gun, 4 x 21-inch and 2 x 18-inch torpedo tubes.
Photo: Goodman Collection.

ABOVE: The Sokol was a U Class submarine (called Urchin in RN service) transferred to the Polish Navy in early 1941. She saw action in the Mediterranean and was returned to the British fleet after the war. BELOW: HMS Vengeful, another U Class boat, was launched in July 1944. Pictured here in late 1944, the following year she was handed over to the Greek Navy and served under its flag for the next 12 years after being re-named Delfin. Photos: Goodman Collection.

ABOVE: HMS United, a Barrow-built boat, which was, together with four other U Class submarines, successful in sinking two German and six Italian submarines in the Mediterranean. In 1942 she also torpedoed and sank the Italian destroyer Bombardiere and submarine Remo. United arrived at Troon for scrapping in January 1946. BELOW: HMS Strongbow, pictured in January 1944, was formerly P235 and was renamed in February 1943. In late 1942, when Prime Minister Winston Churchill found out RN submarines were identified only by numbers, it was ordered that all boats should be given names. Built by Cammell Laird and laid down in March 1942, Strongbow was completed in February the following year. She was scrapped in April 1946. The largest single group of submarines built for the Royal Navy, a total of 62 S Class boats were constructed. In the period 1941-1942 the S Class were fitted with radar sets for surface as well as air search. Using the submarine's ability to operate stealthily, the S Class boats were ideal for secret coastal missions. Note the impressive array of flying boats in the background of this picture. Photos: Goodman Collection.

THE TERRIBLE PRICE PAID

IN FREEDOM'S BATTLE

During WW2 British and Allied submarines were formed into several flotillas or squadrons.

The 1st Flotilla, for example, was composed of British and Greek submarines and patrolled off the harbours of Crete, southern Greece, and the Aegean, largely operating as submersible gunboats.

The most famous British submarine squadron was the so-called Fighting 10th which was based at Malta from 1941 to 1944.

The Fighting 10th included HMS Upholder in which Lieutenant Commander Wanklyn was

ABOVE: The Crew of HM Submarine Splendid assembled on the outer casing of the boat. The CO, Lt Ian McGeoch (later Vice Admiral) is pictured front row, fourth from the left.
BELOW: Splendid again. In April 1943 she was sunk by an enemy destroyer in the Mediterranean. Lt McGeoch survived and, after spending some time in captivity, escaped and made a home run.
Photos: Goodman Collection.

awarded the VC. The Fighting 10th preyed on Italian and German convoys trying to re-supply Axis forces in North Africa. Combined with RAF attacks, the RN's submarines made a significant impact.

Between June 1940, when Italy entered the war, and 1944, British and Allied submarines sank 286 ships totalling 1,030,960 tons, including four cruisers, nine destroyers, eight torpedo-boats and a corvette.

During WW2 the submarine also found a new role, as a submarine hunter-killer and RN boats

accounted for 16 Italian and five German submarines.

The price of victory for the Allies in the Mediterranean was, however, heavy - 45 British, four Greek, two Free French and, after Italy switched sides, one Italian submarine lost.

NEARER home submarines wreaked havoc on German traffic in the Norwegian Inner Leads and midget submarines commenced operations - with much daring and heroism - against Hitler's capital ships in their lairs.

Reinforced in 1944 by boats from the Fighting 10th, patrols by Home Fleet submarines dominated Norwegian waters.

German U-boats were forced to take submerged passage across the North Sea, decreasing their time on active patrol.

AS in the Mediterranean, so it was that for some time in the Far East it was only submarines which could take the offensive for the Royal Navy.

Starting with two boats at Colombo in early 1942, the RN's Eastern submarine force grew over the course of two years to 26. The 10 boats and depot ship of the 8th Flotilla moved to Australia in order to co-operate better with the advancing Americans. None of the S or T boats which served in the Far East had been specifically designed for tropical conditions but they did have air-conditioning.

They also lacked base facilities, and British submarines were, to be blunt, simply inferior to American ones.

The Americans, who had overcome a critical handicap in faulty torpedoes, enjoyed search radar sets, night periscopes with built-in radar, and VHF radios.

As the war drew to a close, the RN's Far East submarines moved to more northerly bases and operated in the waters around

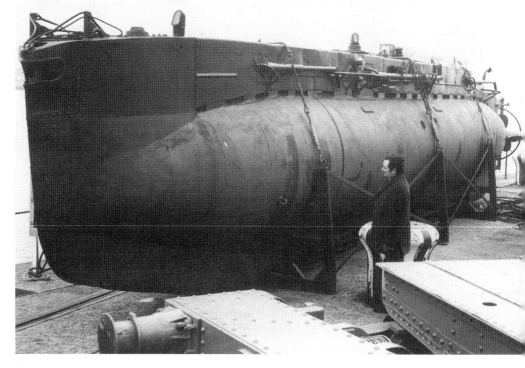

The legendary X craft took part in many daring missions during WW2. In European waters their exploits included an attack on the German battleship Tirpitz in a Norwegian fjord in 1943. They also carried out reconnaissance of the Normandy beaches before the D-Day invasion, and acted as assault route markers for amphibious forces. The XE variants of these highly successful midget submarines were designed for duties in the Far East. They were fitted with air-conditioning and had more storage space than previous X craft. In the Far East XE craft sank the Japanese cruiser Takao in Singapore harbour and cut the communication cables between Singapore and Hong Kong. PICTURED, ABOVE: The XE craft Stickleback, which is now an exhibit at the Imperial War Museum, Duxford. The only surviving X craft on display which saw active service in WW2 is HMS X-24, at the RN Submarine Museum, Gosport. BELOW: XE-12 is pictured at Spithead in January 1951, during the Commonwealth Jubilee Naval Review.
Photos: Goodman Collection.

Singapore, Java, Indo-China and the Philippines, to which the Japanese main naval forces had withdrawn after their expulsion from the Central Pacific.

Targets became increasingly difficult to find, the enemy keeping to shallow coastal waters and creeping along the coast from port to port. Before the end of the war Japan's war industries were starved of essential raw materials from conquered territories and she was unable to send reinforcement to her armies abroad.

By 1945, so successful was the submarine blockade, that in the Pacific, the Indian Ocean and the East Indies there were virtually no targets to be sunk.

ABOVE: HMS Stoic. Launched in March 1943, she was despatched to the Indian Ocean that year. Post-war her rivetted hull was used for deep diving trials. In these a lifting crane lowered her until her hull was crushed by sea pressure, 250ft below maximum operational diving depth. She was sold for scrap in July 1950.
Photo: Goodman Collection.

BELOW: HMS Vitality, which was formerly the Untamed, a modified U Class. She was built at Barrow with a partly welded pressure hull, enabling an increase in operational depth from 200ft to 300ft.
As Untamed she was lost on her trials, in May 1943. Salvaged in July the same year, she was refitted and renamed Vitality. Surviving the war, she was broken up in 1946.
Photo: Goodman Collection.

The submarine, which had been a primitive platform of uncertain use and unknown capability at the beginning of the century, had in WW2 influenced the course of war in three theatres.

It had taken the offensive on occasions when surface ships could not. It had become an effective anti-surface ship and anti-submarine weapon, and, in the East, it had brought Japan's economy to a halt. During WW2, British submarines sunk 1.35 million tons of enemy shipping, including seven cruisers, 16 destroyers, 36 submarines, and 46 minor warships.

They damaged three battleships, 11 cruisers, three destroyers and two submarines.

Out of 25,000 British submariners, 9,310 perished and 359 were taken prisoner.

In WW2 the British submarine service won eight Victoria Crosses for outstanding bravery.

ABOVE: HMS Thorough pictured in February 1944. She was to become a modified T Class after WW2 and was eventually decommissioned and broken up in the early 1960s.
Photos: Goodman Collection.

BELOW: HMS Tally Ho, which notched up an impressive combat record during the closing stages of WW2 in the Far East.
Photo: Goodman Collection.

The
T

The T Class submarines, which saw distinguished service with the Royal Navy during WW2, particularly in the Mediterranean and the Far East, started to enter service at the beginning of the war and were constructed throughout the conflict. HMS Tally Ho (*pictured below*) was laid down in April 1942 and launched in December of the same year. She was completed in April 1943.

Her dimensions were 273' x 26' x 14' and she displaced 1,300 tons surfaced, 1,575 tons submerged. She had a crew of 61.

Her armament was one 4-inch gun and one 20-mm anti-aircraft gun. She had six 21-inch internal torpedo tubes and five 21-inch external torpedo tubes. HMS Tally Ho could manage 15 knots surfaced and 9 knots submerged.

Her career in the Far East was short, but glorious. Between November 1943 and December 31 1944 she sank a Japanese cruiser, a German U-boat, two other minor enemy warships and three cargo vessels. Were it not for defective torpedoes, some of which came back on HMS Tally Ho and only narrowly missed, her score would have been much higher. In early 1944 she was rammed by a Japanese warship while on the surface and that was nearly the end of her. However, Tally Ho managed to escape with ripped ballast tanks and damaged hydroplanes, cautiously setting course for her home base in Ceylon.

In the meantime, the Japanese reported they had sunk her and

rific

ss

her passing was duly mourned. But this turned to cheers when Tally Ho entered Trincomalee harbour on February 29 1944. She found herself surrounded by the newly reformed Eastern Fleet's warships, preparing for offensive operations against the Japanese. Once Tally Ho was in drydock the full extent of her chewed up ballast tanks was visi-

ble. People were amazed she had made it home.

HMS Tally Ho was one of only two Royal Navy submarines to survive ramming by an enemy destroyer in WW2.

She ended her days as a training submarine and was retired from service in 1968.

ANOTHER famous T Class boat was HMS Trenchant which was commissioned at Chatham in early 1944 before setting sail for the Far East.

During her patrols in the Far East she got into many scrapes and

gained fame through sinking the Japanese heavy cruiser Ashigara, reputedly, at 13,000 tons, the largest enemy vessel sunk by a British submarine during WW2. The T Class boats were of course active in other theatres of war, with nearly a dozen sunk during action in the Mediterranean. The T Class submarines managed to notch up an impressive 13 enemy submarines sunk in north European waters, the Mediterranean and the Far East. A number of the class saw service in the Cold War after extensive rebuilds.

ABOVE: The T Class boat HMS Terrapin which became the last British submarine to suffer at the hands of the enemy in WW2. She was badly damaged by depth charges in the Java Sea in May 1945 after attacking a Japanese vessel.

BELOW: HMS Tabard. Launched in November 1945 at Scotts, Greenock, this T Class boat was radically modified post-war and served on until the late 1960s. Photo: Goodman Collection.

LEFT: HMS Sidon was launched in September 1944 at Birkenhead where she was built by Cammell Laird. In June 1955 she suffered severe internal damage when a torpedo fuelled by experimental Hydrogen Peroxide exploded. She ended her days as a target vessel and was sunk off Portland in the summer of 1957.

LEFT, MIDDLE: Two shots of HMS Sentinel surfacing in 5 Basin at Devonport Dockyard during trials. Built by Scott's at Greenock and launched in July 1945, Sentinel was completed too late to take part in the war. Her gun armament was removed when she was fitted with a Snort mast for operational trials. Sentinel was sold on in early 1962.

LEFT, BOTTOM: HMS Totem. Launched at HM Dockyard, Devonport in September 1943, she was one of eight T Class completely rebuilt between 1951-56. In November 1967 Totem was renamed Dakar and taken over on loan by the Israeli Navy. On passage to Haifa from Britain, in January 1968, she was lost in the Eastern Mediterranean with her entire crew of 69. Her wreck was eventually discovered on her plotted course in 1998, by the same civilian team that pinpointed the Titanic and the Bismarck wrecks.
Originally a Totem Pole had been presented to HMS Totem by an Indian tribe and it was said the submarine would be in peril if she ever sailed without it. The Totem Pole is currently at the RN Submarine Museum in Gosport, having been landed by the crew of the Dakar before the boat's fatal final voyage.

Photos: Goodman Collection.

In the late 1940s and 1950s, the cash-strapped Royal Navy was to mainly rely on submarines which had seen service in WW2 or were being built when the conflict ended. Eight T Class boats would be converted between 1951 and 1956, a process which involved cutting them in two so a new section could be inserted. This allowed, among other things, another pair of electric motors and an additional battery section which provided a submerged speed of between 15 and 18 knots. At the same time the A Class submarines under construction in the closing stages of the war were also subjected to an on-going programme of radical modification. As with other leading navies on the winning side in WW2, captured advanced German Type XXI U-boats provided a lot of inspiration, enabling great strides to be taken. The A Class were similar to, but slightly larger than, the Ts and had been designed for war in the

Pacific, carrying more fuel to enable them to cover the vast distances in that theatre of war. Sixteen A Class boats were built, and, following a by now familiar pattern, most of them were

CONSTRUCTED FOR HOT CONFLICT REBUILT FOR A COLD WAR

constructed by Vickers Armstrongs at Barrow, some at one or two other commercial yards plus one at Chatham Dockyard.

The As lasted a long time in British service, their substantial modernisations including removal of their guns and external torpedo tubes, streamlining of the hull, a larger conning tower and new sonars. They had increased battery power for underwater speed and endurance, and were

also fitted with the snorkel breathing device, known as a Snort in the Royal Navy. In their final form, with a surface speed of just under 20 knots and a submerged speed of 8 or 9 knots, the As represented the archetypal diesel powered submarine. Of the class, Aurochs was not modified while Andrew retained her gun after modernisation.

WORK on the first post war British diesel-electric production design, the Porpoise Class, began in 1949. It incorporated all the design modifications already extended to A and T Class conversions. The new submarines were

designed for anti-submarine patrols in the Cold War, and featured stern tubes for short Anti-Submarine torpedoes. The first boat, HMS Porpoise, entered service in 1956, with seven more following.

AT the same time as it pursued the Porpoise programme, the Royal Navy researched the volatile Walther hydrogen-peroxide propulsion system. This, it was hoped, would give high under water speed and enable unrivalled endurance. In the late 1950s two experimental submarines powered by hydrogen-peroxide - HMS Explorer and HMS Excalibur - were constructed. They were not popular boats, as the hydrogen-peroxide was very unstable. With the advent of the nuclear-powered submarine in Russian and the United States fleets, the British abandoned this dangerous research and decided to go atomic as well.

HMS Sceptre was an S Class boat used during WW2 for towing midget submarines. For Operation Source, in September 1943, she towed X-10 over 1,000 miles to the Altenfjord for the attack on the Tirpitz. Sceptre was converted between 1944-45 into a high-speed target submarine for training Anti-Submarine Warfare forces. With hull and casing streamlined, plus gun armament removed, she was given more powerful batteries and motors to replicate the new Type XX1 U-boat the Germans were expected to field in the final stages of the conflict. Sceptre was scrapped in September 1949.
Photo: Goodman Collection.

ABOVE: HMS Selene, completed in July 1944, was by the following year serving in the Far East. In July/August of 1945 Selene towed XE-5, while Spearhead towed XE-4, to positions off Saigon and Hong Kong to cut the Japanese communications cables between Singapore, Saigon and Hong Kong. Selene ended her days as a high-speed target submarine, and was scrapped in the summer of 1961. Photo: Goodman Collection.

BELOW: HMS Andrew, pictured in 1950. She was fitted with an improved Snort in 1951 and made a submerged Atlantic crossing (covering 2,500 miles) in May 1953. After substantial modernisation she was posted to the Far East for 10 years (1958-68). Brought back to UK waters, she was occupied with training ASW forces between 1972 and 1974. Photo: Goodman Collection.

RIGHT: HMS Alcide, pictured in 1947. RIGHT, BELOW: A stern view of Alcide around the same time. Although eleven A Class boats were present at the Coronation Review in 1953, only Alcide remained for the NATO Naval Review 16 years on. She was at the centre of an alert in 1954 when a temporary loss of radio contact gave rise to a widespread search operation. Laid down in January 1945 and completed in October 1946, HMS Alcide was sold in 1974.

RIGHT, MIDDLE: HMS Spiteful (P227), pictured not long after her launch in 1943. She served in the Indian Ocean in 1944. Altered with Snort masts after the war, Spiteful was transferred to the French Navy in the early 1950s and renamed Sirene.
Her career ended with the dawn of the 1960s and she was broken up in 1963.

RIGHT, BOTTOM:
HMS Alliance in the late 1940s. Built by Vickers-Armstrongs and launched in July 1945, Alliance was equipped with 10 torpedo tubes. This consisted of six bow tubes (two external), and four stern tubes (two external). The external tubes were outside the pressure hull, within the free-flood casing, and so could not be reloaded at sea.
Starting at Gibraltar, in early October 1947, Alliance conducted a prolonged tropical Snort cruise lasting 30 days and covered 3,192 miles.

Photos: Goodman Collection.

ABOVE: HMS Alliance today, outside the Submarine Museum, Gosport. Between 1962-66 Alliance undertook operational patrols off Borneo and Indonesia during the confrontation between the UK and Indonesia. In 1965 she was used to test a new camouflage paint scheme in the Far East. She finally paid off in March 1973. The Trustees of the Submarine Museum eventually acquired her from the MoD in 1979. In August that year Alliance was towed to Vospers at Southampton for keel strengthening work. Early the following year she was lifted out of the water and was soon opened to the public. Photo: Dave Cullen.

BELOW: HMS Rorqual and HMS Andrew (right) beached at the breaker's yard, Laira Bridge, Plymouth in 1977. HMS Rorqual was completed by Vickers-Armstrongs in April 1958 and was the second of eight Porpoise Class boats. In 1966 Rorqual was travelling on the surface from Durban to Mombassa, and was off the coast of Mozambique, when a fuel oil separator shattered in the engine-room. The explosion caused no appreciable damage to the submarine, but fatally injured two crewmen.
By the end of 1974, HMS Andrew was the oldest patrol submarine in the Royal Navy, and the last still armed with a deck gun, which was fired for the final time on December 3 1974, a few weeks before her retirement. Photo: Goodman Collection.

Built by Scott's of Greenock and launched in August 1946, the A Class submarine HMS Artemis was not the luckiest of boats.

In 1954 she was the victim of a sabotage incident when a stoker mechanic placed signal grenades in her engines.

On July 2 1971 she sank while alongside at HMS Dolphin, the submarine base at Gosport. Water had entered the boat through an open hatch.

Three of her crew were trapped inside for ten hours. Luckily all three crewmen managed to escape their would-be tomb.

The 1,120 tons submarine was raised on July 6. Retired from service not long after the incident, she was broken up in 1972.

These dramatic photos, showing one of her trapped sailors bobbing to the surface in front of amazed onlookers, above, and the submarine rising to the surface again, left, are by Jonathan Eastland of the renowned AJAX picture library.

ABOVE: HMS Olympus prepares to leave her berth beside HMS Belfast on the Thames in 1982. Launched in 1961, Olympus suffered damage to her conning tower and external superstructure when she was in collision with an unidentified merchant ship while submerged off Portland Bill in December 1978. The last of the unmodernised O Class boats to remain in service, Olympus was paid off for disposal at Gosport in July 1989. Photo: Jonathan Eastland/AJAX.

BELOW: HMS Opossum in floating dock at Devonport Dockyard in the late 1980s. A modified O Class boat, Opossum had an eventful career. She was severely damaged when crash-diving off Land's End, in 1982. She was trying to avoid a Russian spy trawler. She had been shadowing the vessel, when the Russian suddenly changed course toward her and sliced into her fin. Opossum was then badly jarred when she hit the seabed. Later the submarine was brought into Portsmouth under cover of darkness for repairs. Photo: DML.

KEEPING TABS ON THE SOVIETS

The Oberon Class boats quickly followed the successful Porpoise Class submarines.

Thirteen diesel-electric Oberons were completed for the Royal Navy between 1960 and 1967, with another 14 built in the UK for other countries.

These were: Six for Australia (1967-78); three for Canada (1965-68); three for Brazil (1973-77) and two for Chile (1976). Through the peak years of the Cold War, the Ps and Os had hectic careers which only ended recently. The Os were outstanding vessels. Seeing action in Royal Navy service during the 1982 Falklands War and in the

Indian Ocean during the 1991 Gulf conflict, the UK's O boats were only retired from the front line fleet in the early 1990s and in the Canadian and Australian navies were not decommissioned until the end of that decade. Submerged, the O and P Class boats displaced around 2,400 tons and could manage the relatively high speeds of 12 knots (submerged) and 17 knots (surfaced). The Porpoise Class

shared the same outward appearance plus machinery and were the same size as the Os. However, internally the O Class were a considerable improvement. They were quieter than even their stealthy Porpoise predecessors. The O boats' armament consisted of eight torpedo tubes capable of launching Harpoon anti-shipping missiles as well as torpedoes. Despite the advent of nuclear-powered submarines in the 1960s,

diesel-electric boats still had an important role to play.

Their extreme quietness made them ideal for establishing picket lines where they could remain on station for weeks.

As the Soviet submarine fleet grew to over 400 boats in the 1970s and 1980s, the Ps and Os took on the task of loitering along the routes the Soviets would have to use to deploy into the Atlantic.

Often hunting alone, if the Cold War had ever turned hot, they would have easily picked off the advancing enemy.

Their stealth also made them suitable for covert operations.

HMS Opportune is pictured alongside at Devonport in the late 1980s or early 1990s, with a Swiftsure Class SSN to her left and a Fearless Class assault ship looming in the background. Photo: DML.

ABOVE: The Australian O Class submarine HMAS Orion makes an impressive sight out of the water on a shiplift cradle at Transfield. Known as the 'West Coast Warrior', HMAS Orion was under-going a hull clean and painting, systems inspections, plus a routine overhaul, testing and inspection.
Photo: Royal Australian Navy.

BELOW: HMAS Onslow. Commissioned into the Royal Australian Navy in December 1969, Onslow was the fourth of the six Oberon Class boats ordered for the RAN. She was refitted with new fire-control systems between 1982-84 and went operational with Harpoon cruise missiles in December 1984.
Photo: Royal Australian Navy.

O Class boat HMS Osiris, at the Silver Jubilee Review in 1977.
Photo: Jonathan Eastland/AJAX

Another shot of HMS Opportune, this time in drydock at Portsmouth in the mid-1980s.
Photo: Ralph Edwards.

TOP: HMS Odin in 5 Basin at Devonport Dockyard.Photo: DML.

ABOVE: HMS Otter flying a paying off pennant as she sails into Plymouth. In 1964 Otter spent two weeks under the Arctic ice off Greenland, in company with the Porpoise Class submarine Narwhal. Both submarines travelled 600 miles under solid ice 12ft thick, and ran 2,500 miles on soundings. Photo: Mike Welsford.

BELOW: The Canadian O Class boat HMCS Okanagan, pictured in late 1996. Built at Chatham like her sisters - HMCS Ojibwa and HMCS Onondaga - she was the last of the three Oberons to commission into the Royal Canadian Navy (on June 22 1968). Named after Indian tribes, the Canadian O Class boats formed the 1st Canadian Submarine Squadron, based at Halifax. They were retired from service in the late 1990s after Canada signed a long-term leasing deal with the UK for its mothballed Upholder Class boats. See our Upholders article on P47. Photo: Dave Cullen.

ABOVE: The Royal Australian Navy operated six Oberon Class boats between 1967 and 1999. Five of them are pictured above at sea in 1986. Delivery of the original 1963 order for four boats began in 1967 with Oxley. She was followed by Otway in 1968, and Ovens and Onslow in 1969. A further order for two more O Class boats was placed in 1971. Delivery took place during 1977/78, with the Orion and Otama joining the RAN. All the Australian Oberons underwent major refits, starting with Oxley in October 1977, and finishing with Otama in 1985. In their refitted form they were able to carry Harpoon anti-shipping missiles as well as torpedoes. Oxley was stricken in February 1992 and scrapped. Otway was stricken in February 1994 and scrapped in late 1995. Ovens paid off August 1995 and is now a museum exhibit at Fremantle. Orion was decommissioned in September 1996 and placed in reserve at HMAS Stirling for possible emergency reactivation. She was finally sold off in November 1998. Onslow was retired in March 1999 (and is now an exhibit at Sydney). Photo: Royal Australian Navy.

FULL STEAM AHEAD ON NUCLEAR POWER

In the quest for high speeds the Royal Navy had tried steam propulsion in submarines between the world wars, followed in the 1950s and 1960s by the use of hydrogen-peroxide as a fuel. As we have already explained, the latter was too unstable for safe use and so was only ever employed in the experimental boats Explorer and Excalibur.

Developments in nuclear power were to provide the answer. The Americans had built the world's first nuclear-powered submarine, closely followed by the Russians with their own version. The USS Nautilus was a giant of a boat - 3,764 tons surfaced and 4,092 submerged - and could easily exceed 20 knots submerged, which had become something of a barrier for diesel-electric boats. The large hull brought unprecedented comfort for her crew who enjoyed air -conditioning, a juke-box, soda fountain and, for her junior ratings, a mess which could be converted into a cinema with seating for 50. Air for the crew was at first provided by use of oxygen bottles and air scrubbers, direct descendants of systems which had been in use since the late 19th Century and through both world

wars. Soon a revolutionary method of extracting oxygen from seawater was employed. The key to all this was unlimited power from the relatively compact nuclear power plant which drove steam turbines. Steam, it will be remembered, had last been tried in the British K Class. In practice the only limits to the nuclear submarine's endurance were how long her crew could stand being submerged and the length of time it took for food to run out. Nuclear-powered vessels attained a degree of autonomy which warships had not enjoyed since the days of sail.

WHEN the British nuclear power programme fell behind in the late 1950s, Mountbatten - then First Sea Lord - personally intervened to persuade the Americans to sell a complete power plant from one of their Skipjack submarines. Interestingly, in the early staff papers concerning these developments, the nuclear power plant

was referred to as the "re-actor". The new British nuclear submarines were too large to use Haslar Creek at Gosport, where submarines had been based since the beginning of the century, and instead were based at Devonport, Chatham, Rosyth and a new base at Faslane on the east coast of Scotland.

THE Royal Navy was deeply self-conscious about the significance of its first nuclear submarine. Named Dreadnought, she reminded the world, and perhaps the Navy itself, that she was every bit as revolutionary as Fisher's all-big-gun battleship had been in 1906. Next came the Valiant Class nuclear-powered attack boats (SSNs). The first Polaris ballistic missile submarines (SSBNs) were the R (Resolution) Class, the current nuclear-powered attack submarines are S (Swiftsure) and T (Trafalgar) Class. The Royal Navy's final class of

diesel-electric boats were the U (Upholder) Class and the present Trident ballistic missile submarines are the V (Vanguard) Class. The end of the alphabet has been missed, and the new generation of attack boats being built at the moment for the Royal Navy will belong to the A (Astute) Class.

THE nuclear submarine is a unique tool of naval diplomacy, able to sail either covertly or in a blaze of publicity, depending on the circumstances. In the late 1970s the overt deployment of an SSN (nuclear attack boat) to the South Atlantic deterred the Argentineans enough to prevent an invasion of the Falklands. However, in 1982, this did not happen and the Argentineans were bold enough to actually carry out an invasion. In the subsequent war the presence of nuclear submarines and, in the case of the Belgrano sinking, their power being demonstrated, was instrumental in keeping the enemy's main fleet in port.

IN the late 1980s the Royal Navy decided that its optimum submarine force should be 16 nuclear-powered vessels (12 SSNs and four

Continued on p40

The cruise missile-armed Swiftsure Class submarine HMS Splendid is pictured in July 2000, at buoy in Plymouth Sound
Photo: Mike Welsford.

PICTURED OPPOSITE, BELOW:
The Valiant Class nuclear attack boat HMS Valiant arriving at Portsmouth in June 1968.
Photo: Jonathan Eastland/AJAX.

SSBNs) and eight diesel-electric patrol submarines.

However, the post-Cold War defence cuts meant that first this was scaled back to just four diesel-electric boats plus the nuclear-powered vessels.

Then the four diesels were retired from service altogether and have now been acquired on long-term lease by the Canadian fleet.

The Royal Navy submarine force of today is an all-nuclear one.

• *For more detail on topics covered in this scene-setting article see articles on following pages.*

TOP: HMS Valiant (right) and the Dutch diesel-electric submarine HNLMS Zwaardis at Plymouth Navy Days, 1977. HMS Valiant was the first all-British nuclear-powered submarine.
Photo: Goodman Collection.

MIDDLE: An impressive shot of the Trafalgar Class SSN HMS Triumph leaving Plymouth in 1997, headed north for exercise waters off the west coast of Scotland.
Photo: Nigel Andrews.

BOTTOM: Triumph drops off the Pilot before heading out beyond the Plymouth Sound breakwater.
Photo: Nigel Andrews.

LEFT: HMS Triumph at speed on the surface off the Lizard. Photo: Nigel Andrews.

BELOW: The Triumph two years earlier, during an August 1995 visit to Portsmouth.
HMS Triumph is the newest nuclear submarine in the British front line fleet, having been commissioned in 1992. Photo: Dave Cullen.

RIGHT, TOP: HMS Triumph noses through waters off England's South West Peninsula.

RIGHT, MIDDLE: Later, as she transits the Irish Sea on the surface, her Officer of the Watch scans the horizon.

RIGHT, BOTTOM: After diving in the Irish Sea, Triumph's planesman - a medic getting some additional vocational training - awaits his orders.

BELOW: The sharp end - HMS Triumph's torpedo tubes are an engineering marvel.

All Photos: Nigel Andrews.

FROM DREADNOUGHT TO TRAFALGAR

Although in 1958 a reactor was bought from the United States to power the Royal Navy's first nuclear attack boat (SSN) - HMS Dreadnought - a larger, British, reactor went into the second boat, HMS Valiant, two years later. Valiant was therefore slightly larger than Dreadnought in order to accommodate this change.

Nuclear-powered but conventionally armed, these new attack submarines were designed to operate in close support of a task force or a convoy. Five SSNs - also known as Fleet Submarines - of the Valiant Class were built between 1966 and 1971.

Of the Valiant Class, HMS Conqueror was the most famous. On returning from her war patrol off the Falklands in 1982, she flew the skull and crossbones flag to indicate she had drawn blood. Her attack on the Argentinean cruiser Belgrano off the Falklands was carried out to protect the UK task force sent to liberate the islands. Although the former US Navy cruiser was elderly she was fitted with Exocet missiles and could have killed many British sailors, if they had been launched. When Conqueror first sighted the Belgrano and her escorting destroyers they were taking on fuel from a tanker.

From the moment first contact was established HMS Conqueror kept the Belgrano group under a tight watch via periscope and sonar.

On the attack run Conqueror closed to 1,400 yards and used three Mark 8 WW2-vintage torpedoes. The older weapons were well proven and Conqueror's Tigerfish torpedoes were suffering teething problems.

The Conqueror was in the perfect attacking position, at right-angles to the target.

The torpedoes did their deadly work and the Belgrano sank with large loss of life, partly due to the fact that many of the vessel's water-tight doors were open, despite being in a war situation. The fact that the Belgrano and her escorts were making no attempt to use sonar also left the cruiser very vulnerable. After her brief moment of fame, Conqueror's activities were once more plunged into deliberate obscurity as she went back to the old game of cat-and-mouse with the Russians.

WITH the decision to purchase the Polaris A3 missile from the United States in 1963, work on ballistic missile boats (SSBNs) of the Resolution Class had commenced in 1964, with the first completed in 1967.

These boats were based on the US Navy's Lafayette Class, but with British equipment and machinery.

A major external difference was the British decision to position the forward hydroplanes on the bows rather than the fin. In addition to their Polaris missiles, these boats carried conventional torpedoes, and were therefore fitted with six tubes. The four boats of the class - Resolution, Repulse, Renown and Revenge - entered service between 1967 and 1969, and eventually replaced the strategic deterrent of the RAF bomber force.

WHEN it came to new SSNs, the first boat of the Swiftsure Class was completed in 1973. Designed as a successor to the Valiant Class, six Swiftsures had been built by 1980. Proving particularly successful, the Swiftsure Class led to the Trafalgar Class attack submarine.

Keeping to the same basic hull-form and lay-out, the Trafalgars incorporate advances in electronics and acoustic detection methods.

The drive system on the Trafalgars employs hydrojets, rather than the conventional 7-bladed propellers, to reduce noise.

Albeit only 8ft longer than the Swiftsures, the Trafalgar boats have an increased submerged displacement. With the first commissioned in 1983, there are now seven boats of this class of SSN.

The Trafalgar Class SSN HMS Trenchant heads out of Plymouth Sound in the summer of 1999. She is sporting striking pale blue stripes on her outer casing, allegedly to disguise her better during shallow water operations.
Photo: Nigel Andrews.

ABOVE: HMS Trafalgar alongside at Devonport in the mid-1990s. Launched in 1981, she was the first of the Trafalgars which are a stretched version of the Swiftsure Class. They are faster, can dive deeper, and run quieter than their predecessors. With the retro-fitting of Tomahawk alongside Harpoon missiles, and the latest torpedoes, their punch is formidable. Photo: DML.

BELOW: The Resolution Class ballistic missile submarine HMS Renown navigating the channel in Plymouth Sound, in April 1971, possibly the only visit by a Polaris SSBN to the Devon naval port. Renown was paid off in 1996. The successors to the R Class boats, the V Class SSBNs, will definitely be regular visitors to Plymouth as they are to be refitted at Devonport Dockyard, with the first arriving in 2002. Photo: Ridolfo/Goodman.

HMS Triumph on the surface in the mouth of the Clyde. Photo: Nigel Andrews.

The Royal Navy operates four Vanguard Class Trident ballistic missile submarines (SSBNs) - HMS Vanguard, HMS Victorious, HMS Vigilant and HMS Vengeance. Carrying 16 Trident D5 missiles, these awesome boats are expected to provide the UK's nuclear deterrent umbrella for the next 20 years at least. As with their Polaris-carrying predecessors, two crews of 135 sailors - a starboard and a port watch - ensure that the RN's SSBNs are out on patrol constantly, providing protection for Britain 365 days a year. A relaxation of Vanguard Class operating procedures was announced in the UK's 1998 Strategic Defence Review, enabling the SSBNs to be allowed to work on a less restrictive leash. They now undertake secondary tasks while on patrol, including hydrographic data collection, equipment trials and exercises with other vessels.

Photo: Iain Ballantyne.

ABOVE: The Upholder Class submarine HMS Ursula taking part in the D-Day 50th anniversary fleet review off Portsmouth in June 1994. Photo: Ralph Edwards.

BELOW: HMS Unicorn arrives back at Plymouth in late 1994 to pay off after her global voyage. Photo: Nigel Andrews (who also took the impressive head on shot of Unicorn, opposite).

The Upholders
Last of a Breed

HMS Upholder had one of the shortest careers of any submarine in the Royal Navy, and her enemy was not the Russians or the Germans, but the UK Treasury. She was added to the Royal Navy's post-Cold War fleet in 1990, and three others - Unseen, Ursula and Unicorn - had joined her at Devonport Naval Base by early 1994. The class had cost some £1 billion to build. Completed between 1989 and 1993, they were constructed at Barrow by VSEL and at Birkenhead by Cammell Laird. Their displacement was 2,400 tons submerged and they could manage 20 knots dived. Their crews varied between 44 and 49 sailors. They were fitted with six torpedo tubes which could fire torpedoes and Harpoon anti-shipping missiles. By the end of 1994 none of the Upholders were in service and the submarine flotilla had gone all-nuclear. When the last Upholder to remain in service - HMS Unicorn (*see pictures, left & right*) - returned to Devonport in October 1994, after a global deployment, she represented the end of the diesel-electric era for the Royal Navy, which had started 93 years before with the Hollands. The Upholders were comparable in all aspects of performance, except underwater speed, to any nuclear boat. Their quietness was legendary.

HMS Unicorn's last operational voyage for the Royal Navy, to the Indian Ocean and Persian Gulf, was a highly acclaimed, successful, un-supported long range deployment, giving the vessel's 49 crew invaluable experience. She soon joined her three sisters at the VSEL yard in Barrow. They were laid-up until 1998, when the Canadian and UK governments agreed a long-term leasing deal, which sees them crossing the Atlantic to serve in the Canadian fleet as the Victoria Class.

ROYAL NAVY PLANS AN ASTUTE FUTURE

From modest beginnings a century ago, the submarine arm of the Royal Navy progressed swiftly to win its spurs in two world wars. Through the Cold War, while the Royal Navy shrank in size, the credibility of its submarine arm remained intact. Today it is not only respected by allies such as the US Navy, but feared by potential adversaries. Today the RN's huge ballistic missile submarines are pre-eminent capital warships, carrying nuclear-tipped weapons which can lay waste to entire continents. It is to be hoped that one day mankind can mutually agree to rid itself of all atomic weapons and send these vessels to the scrapyard along with the SSBNs of America, Russia, China and France. But, while the Cold War 'balance of terror' is history, we have entered an era where many previously non-nuclear countries are arming themselves with Weapons of Mass Destruction (WMD). Among these new nuclear powers, India aspires to field its own 21st Century capital ship by constructing a new type of SSBN.

THE Vanguard Class SSBNs of the British fleet will continue for another two decades at least to represent Britain's best protection against the rising WMD threat. New Astute Class attack boats (SSNs) will shortly be acting as

'battle-cruiser' escorts to the SSBN 'battleships'. The keel of the first in a batch of three new A Class attack boats - HMS Astute - was laid at Barrow at the beginning of 2001. She is being constructed in sections and will be the largest attack boat yet built for the Royal Navy, at 7,200 tonnes (dived). The three already ordered - Astute, Ambush and Artful - will be followed by a further batch of two or three units. The Astutes will be replacing the Swiftsure Class and the early Trafalgar Class boats. In the wake of the 1998 Strategic Defence Review (SDR), the RN will maintain a force of just 10 SSNs, down from 18 in the final years of the Cold War. A contract for the second batch of A Class SSNs is expected in 2002 and in the meantime Astute herself is due to be launched in 2004 and commissioned the following year. As well as being 40 per cent larger than her predecessors, Astute will operate with about ten per cent fewer people, but have a substantially increased weapon load, including a sixth torpedo tube. This allows greater flexibility in weapon load when choosing between Spearfish torpedoes, Harpoon anti-shipping missiles or Tomahawk Land-Attack Missiles (TLAMs). With room for about double the number of weapons of existing submarines, an Astute

Class boat will be able to remain on-task for much longer. When HMS Splendid fired Tomahawks in the Kosovo operation of 1999, she had to return to port at least twice to re-arm. The new boats will also have a more powerful nuclear reactor propulsion plant than earlier SSNs, using the same basic design as that already at sea in the Vanguard Class SSBNs. According to the builders, BAE SYSTEMS Marine (formerly Vickers), the larger boat is actually cheaper to construct than a smaller unit similar to the earlier classes. The improved capabilities of the new class will go some way to compensate for the large reduction in numbers of attack submarines in RN service. After Astute will come the Future Attack Submarine, which will aim to build on the significant advances of the A Class.

A FLEET with SSNs has a truly global reach and, with all UK SSNs being fitted with Tomahawk, a powerful influence over events on land can be exerted via precision strikes. As the battleships of the 19th and 20th Centuries were able to sit off a hostile shore and carry out bombardments - 'gunboat diplomacy' - so the cruise missile-armed SSNs of the RN and USN are able to fire on strategic targets today. Diesel-electric boats (SSKs) do still

have their uses and those navies which possess them consider them to be their capital ships. SSKs are generally quieter than nuclear-powered boats. They can close shipping lanes as efficiently as an SSN by their mere presence without necessarily needing to sink a ship. The influence of a trio of Russian-built Kilo Class SSKs in the Gulf, and the amount of effort put into countering the residual threat of Serb-crewed submarines, by NATO in the Adriatic in 1999, was clear evidence of the potency of conventional boats. If the Royal Navy wants to continue to preserve the freedom of the seas, and its own freedom of manoeuvre, then it must maintain its anti-submarine forces. Submarines make the best anti-submarine weapons. In its submarine flotilla are skills in which the Royal Navy leads the world. It is a lead which it must not lose.

NUCLEAR-POWERED attack submarines possess stealth, speed, and endurance. They can be used in a variety of scenarios and have the versatility to switch roles swiftly. They can easily gain access to crisis points via the two thirds of the world covered in water. Their suitability for joint and multi-national operations, at all levels of warfare, means that submarines are here to stay.